Carpentry and Exterior Finish

"Approaches the subject in a casual, uncomplicated, humorous way and has solutions to many unforeseen problems. [But] don't misunderstand; this is a serious book. . . ."

—*1,001 Home Ideas*

"Ever wish some 'old-timer' house builder who really knew construction inside and out would help you avoid all the little (and big!) glitches you're likely to run into when you're finally ready to build your own home? Well, that's exactly what Bob Syvanen has done."

—*The Mother Earth News*

"An excellent resource for the homebuilder."

—*The Counselor*

by Bob Syvanen

Drafting: Tips and Tricks on
Drawing and Designing House Plans

Carpentry and Exterior Finish: Some Tricks of the Trade

Carpentry and Interior Finish: More Tricks of the Trade

Getting a Good House:
Tips and Tricks for Evaluating New Construction

HOME BUILDER'S LIBRARY, VOLUME TWO

Carpentry and Exterior Finish:

Some Tricks of the Trade from an Old-Style Carpenter

Third Edition

by Bob Syvanen

The Globe Pequot Press

Old Saybrook, Connecticut

Library of Congress Cataloging-in-Publication Data

Syvanen, Bob.
    Carpentry and exterior finish : some tricks of the trade / by Bob
Syvanen. -- 3rd ed.
       p. cm. -- (Home builder's library ; v. 2)
     Rev. ed. of : Carpentry, some tricks of the trade. 2nd ed. 1988.
     ISBN 1-56440-078-6
     1. House construction. 2. Carpentry. 3. Exterior walls.
 I. Syvanen, Bob. Carpentry, some tricks of the trade.
 II. Title. III. Series.
TH54811.S97   1993
694--dc20
                                                     93-2371
                                                      CIP

Manufactured in the United States of America
Third Edition/First Printing

Contents

Foreword

During my forty years as an architect, I have dealt with hundreds of contractors, builders, carpenters, and cabinetmakers. Many have done better than average work; a few have been outstanding. Seeing variations, I've often wondered what it was that made one person's work so much better than another's. It didn't seem to depend on intelligence, exactly, or experience, or even manual skills. Not completely. There was something else involved. But it wasn't until I watched Bob Syvanen build my house that the answer began to dawn upon me.

There is a direct relationship between good carpentry and efficient work habits. Skilled carpenters seem to produce less waste. They waste less time, less effort, and fewer materials. They turn mistakes to their advantage. They know the tricks of the trade.

After I'd seen Bob in action for several months, I asked him if he'd consider doing a book on his craft—not on carpentry as such (the market is flooded with good books on that subject) but on the little secrets that spell the difference between crisis-to-crisis carpentry and under-control carpentry. As soon as Bob agreed, I talked him into giving me the illustrating job.

It may seem slightly inappropriate to see so many pages devoted to ordinary carpentry when the world is running out of fuel, when newer, more efficient, kinds of buildings are so badly needed. You might think we should be offering information instead on, say, solar-house construction. But the market is flooded with good books on that subject, too.

No matter what we build we must learn to build it efficiently, to do it right in spite of all the junk that passes for building materials today. That's what Bob's book is all about.

MALCOLM WELLS

Preface

The older I get, the more I am convinced that anyone can do anything. All we need is enough desire.

In any endeavor there are the little unforeseen problems that can cause us to stumble; and although there are many how-to books on all manner of subjects, these little unforeseen problems are rarely mentioned. How we deal with these problems is frequently what makes for a success or failure in our efforts.

We read about joists and rafters. We learn where they go, how many nails. But what shall I do when the wood is warped and doesn't do what it is supposed to do? Is there an easy way to pick up lumber and walk with it? Mistakes occur; and although they are not in themselves bad, they do cause us to stumble.

Mistakes are just a different way of doing something—and with a different consequence. Many times a so-called mistake turns out to be the effort with the better consequence. These "mistakes" (of which I have made quite a few) are great learning tools. How we deal with them is what separates the good from the mediocre. When a problem occurs, stay loose; the solution is always there.

I got into carpentry forty years ago because I wanted to be a good architect. I wanted to know about the little problems and their solutions. So for forty years I have been learning to be a carpenter and architect, and my hope for this book is that it will make at least one job easier for someone.

Remember two things:

1. Measure twice, cut once.
2. You are building a house, not a piano.

Species of lumber can cause problems, but we can overcome. There are five basic choices:

1. Douglas fir
2. Southern or yellow pine
3. Spruce
4. Hemlock
5. Native pine (New England)

Douglas Fir

Number-one choice, along with yellow pine, for framing. When I first started, fir is all I ever saw. It is strong, straight, heavy, and hard. It is highly decay resistant, making it ideal for foundation sills and decks. The problems with fir come from the fact that it is heavy and hard. On some old charts fir was listed as a hardwood. There are five things to be aware of when working with fir:

1. It is heavy.
2. It is hard to cut with a handsaw, particularly a dull handsaw.
3. It is hard to nail.
4. It splits easily.
5. It has bleeding pitch pockets.

Solutions:
1. It's heavy, so get strong.
2. The handsaw is not used as much as in the past, so that presents less of a problem. There are times, however, when it must be used. Make sure it is sharp, and cut with a slow, steady stroke. Be sure the stock is well supported and steady.
3. Good nailing just takes practice and a strong forearm. Before I started my first job, I used to practice nailing every day. I also squeezed a rubber ball to improve my grip.
4. Avoid nailing too close to the end of a board. Don't use a 16d nail when an 8d will do.
5. Bleeding pitch pockets are hard to control. They pose no problem if the lumber is used as a stud or joist; but if it is used as an exposed beam, there could be trouble. Look for a brown spot or streak, especially a crack with the tell-tale brown. Use it with the blemish turned up to keep it from dripping pitch on whatever is below. Sometimes such spots can be cut out and patched, but beware: The pocket can be quite extensive.

Southern or Yellow Pine

Handles like fir but without the pitch pockets. It, too, is heavy, straight, and strong. It also has a lot of resin, which bleeds through paint.

Solution:
Same as for fir. Try different sealers on samples before painting.

Spruce

Spruce seems to be the most common framing lumber on the East Coast. It is very light (particularly when dry), easy to cut, and easy to nail, and it sounds wonderful. It does have three weak points:

1. Low decay resistance
2. Poor nail holding
3. Weak

Solutions:
1. Avoid using where moisture is a problem, such as sills and outdoor decks. If it must be used where moisture is present, paint and protect with overhanging or capping sheets of metal. Use pressure-treated lumber for foundation sills.
2. Use adequate nailing, preferably hot-dipped galvanized nails.
3. Use proper sized timber for design loads on building.

Hemlock

Hemlock and spruce seem to be what we are offered these days (in New England, at least) for framing. Hemlock, when dry, is quite hard and tends to split. It also twists badly—great if you are making skis. Hemlock has one good quality that I know of. It is a good match for birch and can be used as trim with birch cabinets and doors. It stains similar to birch, but test a few samples first. Hemlcok can be recognized by the natural blue streaks in the wood.

Solutions:
1. Use when green, and nail it quick before it gets away.
2. Do not use for outdoor decks.

Native Pine

Native pine of New England is good to work with but getting scarce. Only the small mills cut it. It, too, is highly decay resistant.

⏱ Lumber Finishes and Seasoning

The differences in the species and condition of your lumber can cause problems. There are four condition choices:

1. *Air dry or kiln dry, dressed.* Kiln dry should have less moisture content at the end of the drying process. Air dry takes four months to a year, depending on size. Kiln dry takes one-fourth the time. Both are planed smooth. The mark on the lumber will be "S-Dry" or "Kiln Dry."

2. *Green dressed.* Freshly cut and planed smooth, full of moisture. The mark will be "S-Green."

3. *Green rough cut.* Freshly cut. Rough exterior, full of moisture. No mark; the surface is too rough to take a stamp.

4. *Dry rough cut.* Rough exterior, usually air dry. No marks, too rough. It is very easy, by the weight of the lumber, to tell if it is dry.

Some other marks you will see are "D" for dry and "M.C. 15%" for moisture content 15 percent.

Air Dry or Kiln Dry, Dressed

This is the easiest to work with. Mixing air dry and kiln dry causes problems, though, if the air dry has been drying for too short a time. The dimensions of this lumber will be larger than those of the kiln dry, and if you use them together—problems.

Solution:

Use either the kiln dried or the air dried. When using differing dimensioned lumber, you are constantly compensating by shimming up or trimming off (and sometimes forgetting). If using both kiln and air dried, do your compensating act, and use the material where it will matter the least, like rafters.

Green Dressed

Four problems here:

1. It is heavy.
2. Lumber will shrink.
3. Rotting and fungus are encouraged.
4. It does not show pencil mark well.

Solutions:

1. The weight of green lumber can be overcome. Go on a good weight-lifting program. One man can lift one 2"x10"x16' green plank; two can be handled if dry.

2. Years ago the framed house dried in the summer sun. It can still be done that way, or a few portable heaters can be used. Practice good fire-prevention methods. Provide ventilation to remove moisture from house as it is driven from the lumber.

3. Separate layers of lumber with sticks as soon as it is delivered. Use 1-inch sticks for thin boards and 2-inch for thick boards.

Use an indelible pencil for marking wet lumber, but beware of "blue temple." If you carry the pencil behind the ear, it will leave its mark each time.

Dry Rough

The big problem here is the uneven dimensions. A 2x4 may measure 2"x4" at one end and 2⅛"x2¼" at the other. A 1x6 could be 1½" and ⅞". The larger dimensions vary not only from end to end but also from timber to timber. One may measure 9¾"; another, 10¼". The better mills have better, but not absolute, control. That is one of the reasons for dressing lumber. It is easier to control the finished size with a planer.

Solution:

Be aware of variations and compensate by shimming and trimming. Use where it matters least.

Green Rough

Green rough has the same problems as dry rough, with the added bonus of heavy and more shrinkage.

Solution:

Be aware of variations and start a real good weight-lifting program.

All these methods will move lumber, but not without wasting time and energy. None of these show good control, so they are not safe. A man at each end will make easy work of the job, but it will also take twice as long.

Picking up a single piece of lumber is not a big problem, but forty 2x10s are. The best way to carry lumber is on the shoulder, and the quickest is "the lazy man's load," two at a time (twenty trips instead of forty). If the lumber is green, even two might be a bit much to handle. When the load is carried on the shoulder, the sticks must point in the direction you are walking. When carried at waist level, the load is perpendicular to the direction you are walking and the way of the legs. If two boards are carried that way, though, they will scissor.

To pick up a load properly, stand as close to the load as possible with knees bent and back straight. The arms will hang straight at the elbows, with the left hand reaching over to grab the forward edge of the load and the right hand grabbing the rear of the load, thumbs up. With the arms straight and the back kept flat, the powerful leg muscles do the lifting. Don't jerk the load off the ground or the back will bend. Instead, drive hard with the legs; and, as you pass your knees, shrug your shoulders hard. When the load is as high as it will go, drop under it, and at the same time, pivot the body and both feet to the left 90 degrees while rolling the load to catch on the shoulder. The lumber face that was up is now down. To cushion the load as it lands on the shoulder, raise the right arm up and forward. The load will then land on the shoulder muscle instead of the bone. Balance the load by bouncing it off the shoulder and quickly shifting under it. Once the load is balanced, only the right arm, raised and stretched forward on top of the load, is needed for control as you walk.

Back and arms
straight . . .

A shrug with the
shoulders . . .

Pivot, dip, and onto
the right shoulder
with right arm raised . . .

The lift is complete ("three white lights," as they say in
weightlifting), and you are on your way.

The load can be tossed from one shoulder to the other by thrusting with the legs. To drop
the load either roll it off your shoulder onto your right forearm or toss it up and away
with a leg thrust. Practice right and left shoulder with a few light boards.

Moving sheets of plywood or Sheetrock is not one of your fun jobs, but there is a better way than shown here.

This is awkward. The weight of the sheet is not well distributed, and walking is difficult.

This position is best; the weight is carried on the bottom hand. The top hand keeps the sheet from tipping.

It's a struggle when two people carry one sheet using opposing grips. Each person should have the same carrying hand down (right hand for righties, as shown above).

How the lumber is stacked and where it sits on the building site can be great helps in minimizing problems. When making a list for the yard, indicate what the materials are for. Be sure to keep a copy for yourself. The lumber yard will then be able to stack the lumber on the truck in a good sequence. Sometimes yards do a good job and sometimes not. At any rate it should be stacked with the building sequence in mind.

LUMBER LIST		
EXTERIOR STUDS	2 x 6	400/8'
INTERIOR STUDS	2 x 4	420/8'
FIRST FLOOR JOISTS	2 x 10	50/14'
HEADERS	2 x 10	7/12' 10/14'
SECOND FLOOR JOISTS	2 x 10	50/14'

When ordering lumber, don't forget to order at least a half-dozen extra 2"x10"x14' planks for scaffolding. Also get two or three bundles of cheap wood shingles for shimming, two dozen 1"x6"x16' fence board (an inexpensive board for bracing), and two bundles of 1x3 furring strips for bracing.

Before the lumber truck arrives, think about what problems the stack of lumber will cause:

1. Ease of access for truck
2. Ease of unloading
3. Restacking of load
4. Moving lumber from stack to building
5. Location of radial saw and power pole
6. Masonry supplies
7. Traffic flow

Green timber should be stacked crisscrossed and thin boards stacked with 1-inch spacers. Align spacers vertically or thin boards will dry curved. Keep all good lumber off the ground. In the Alpine countries, timber stacks were dried for three years before use. The thin boards were stored for one year.

Plywood can be secured by nailing the corners down with 16d nails for half or more of the stack. It helps keep the stack from walking away. Removing nails in the dark is difficult and noisy. Cover with plastic and plenty of wood strips.

Kiln dry lumber should be covered with a tarp; plastic works well. Use plenty of wood strips nailed through the plastic to the stack inside. This cover keeps the rain, snow, and sun off and makes it difficult for this lumber to walk off. I once built a plywood wall around a stack of lumber to keep it from disappearing.

PLOP PLOP PLOP....

Stand rolls of building paper under cover on their ends on a piece of plywood. Rolls that lay on their sides get oval shaped and don't unroll too easily. If they sit on the ground the ends pick up dirt and moisture, again making unrolling difficult.

When using temporary posts, cut them about three-quarters of an inch shorter than they should be. It is a simple job to shim up with wood shingles. Use any jacking device available to raise the beam: hydraulic, screw, or auto—even a lever.

It is easier to put the post on the footing with the jack on top. If the jack is on the bottom, the post then has to be balanced on the jack with one hand while you work the jack with the other. Of course with two people, either way will work.

The temporary posts can be secured with a brace each way. Once floor joists are in, the braces can be removed.

Columns and Posts

Lally columns are concrete-filled steel tubes. The easiest way to cut them is with a large tubing cutter. Most lumber yards have them and will cut the columns, but you take a chance on their accuracy. The best thing to do is to measure them up, deduct for the top and bottom plates, take them to the yard, and cut them yourself. If they come up a little short, metal shims will bring them up.

You can also cut them on the job with a hacksaw. The ends are always square, so just mark the length four or five places around the column.

Cut most of the way through the metal case all around.

Raise the cut end and rest on a block or another column.

Smack with sledge . . . presto.

When shimming the ends of beams resting on concrete or steel, use a non-compressible material like steel, slate, or asbestos board. Asbestos board works well because it comes in ⅛-inch sheets, which makes it easy to build up, and it cuts easily.

SHIM
BELOW BEAM

The shims are to keep the beam up permanently, and if wood is used, it will shrink, compress, and maybe even rot away. Plywood works pretty well; its compression loss is minimal.

Sills are the most important step in the building. If all is square and level, then the rest will go quite easily.

Steps for Setting Sills

1. Establish true and square corners.
2. Establish the inside corners of sills.
3. Mark inside edge of sills.
4. Select material for sills.
5. Locate anchor bolt holes on sill; drill.
6. Set sills in place.
7. Level sills.
8. Install termite barrier.

Establishing True and Square Corners

After the foundation has been completed, check its length and width against the plan. If sides are equal and diagonals are equal, then the foundation is square. If not, an adjustment must be made.

50'-0"
50'-0"
40'-0"
30'-0"

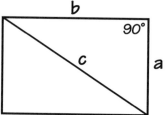

The exact diagonal can be found mathematically ($a^2+b^2=c^2$); and with small pocket calculators, it is easy. There are special slide rules that give the diagonal with a twist of a dial. Just keep adjusting corners until you hit the dimensions required.

If you have a foundation that is more than a simple rectangle, the 3, 4, 5 triangle is very helpful. After the main foundation is squared, an addition can be squared off any wall with the 3, 4, 5 triangle. The 3, 4, 5 triangle is the same as $a^2+b^2=c^2$ ($3^2 + 4^2 = 5^2$).

When the corners are established, mark them on the foundation. If a corner is ½ inch outside of the concrete, mark ½" ↑. If it is ½ inch in on the concrete, mark ½" ←. If an edge is right on, mark "good."

True Inside Corner

Take a short block of the sill material and place it at the corner, the true outside corner. Mark the inside face on the foundation. Use a nail to scratch a good mark each way forming a "+" for the true inside corner.

Mark Inside Edge of Sills

With corners marked, snap a red chalk line connecting the inside corners. This is the inside edge of the sill; use it for control. It doesn't matter what the foundation does. Red chalk shows up better on concrete, but blue will do.

RED CHALK LINE

ENLARGED DETAIL OF THIS CORNER BELOW

Material for Sills

The best is pressure treated; and, in fact, many areas of the country require its use.
Douglas fir is the next choice because of its high decay resistance. Any other wood is all right if moisture is kept away. Choose straight pieces.

Locate Anchor Bolts

Rest the sill on the foundation alongside bolts at its proper location relative to the true outside corner. With a combination square, locate and mark the center line of bolts.

CHALK LINE

FOR 2x6 SILL: 5½"

SQUARE

PENCIL LINE

5½" WIDE 2x6 SILL

ANCHOR BOLTS

Measure from center line of bolts to chalk line, transfer to sill. Drill ⅝-inch hole for ½-inch bolt to allow for adjusting.

2½"

2¾"

2½"

2¾"

There are usually a few anchor bolts leaning . . .

To straighten, beat them over with a hand maul, but screw a nut on and hit it instead of the bolt threads.

Locating anchor-bolt holes is easy with this tool. Align the outside face of the sill with the chalk line. With the tool in place, hammering on the shelf-tapping screw locates the bolt hole.

5 ½"

5 ½"

5 ½"

5 ½"

EYEBALL 90°

CHALK LINE AT INSIDE EDGE OF MUDSILL

5 ½"
FOR A 2x6

ANCHOR BOLT

DOWEL HANDLE

BLADE FROM COMBINATION SQUARE

SELF-TAPPING SCREW MARKS LOCATION OF ANCHOR-BOLT HOLE

Sills

Installing Sills

Lightly bolt the first corner sill piece in place, lining up with the inside corner chalk line and the true outside corner. The next piece is then butted up against it, and the same procedure is followed for bolt locations. When all the sill pieces are in place, recheck lengths, widths, and diagonals. Adjust if necessary.

Leveling Sills

The most accurate tool for leveling is the water tube level. It is just a long piece of clear plastic tubing with a colored antifreeze solution in it. There are garden hose attachments available, but the problem with a garden hose is that you can't see if the line is clear of bubbles. The line must be clear or you will not get a true reading.

Using the tube is very simple. Keep one end at the high point of the foundation and move the other to various points around the wall. The water will seek the same level at each end, and you can note the variations in wall heights. Mark these height differences on the wall: + ½", - ¼", and so on.

½" LOW

SIGHT LINE

LEVEL LINE

INSTRUMENT OUT OF LEVEL

The builder's level is good as long as care is taken when setting up. Try to keep the "shots" short. The further away from the instrument, the greater the error.

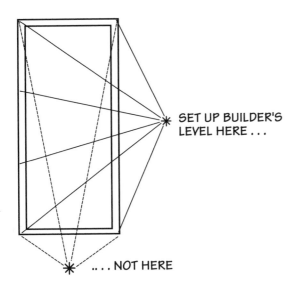

SET UP BUILDER'S LEVEL HERE . . .

. . . . NOT HERE

The instrument can be set up inside, at the center, of a low foundation wall to good advantage. When shooting from outside, set up along the long wall to keep "shots" short and somewhat equal.

CRAWL SPACE

Set up a reference point that you can check easily. Someone is bound to kick one of the tripod legs. You can use a nail in a tree or some stationary object, a ruler, or a wood soldier.

SOLDIER

RULE

NAIL

3"(EXAMPLE)

FOUNDATION WALL

As long as the cross hairs hit the original reference mark (nail in tree, mark on ruler, mark on wood soldier), all is well. If the instrument is moved, a new reference point must be established. Keep checking. There is an old carpenter's saying: "measure twice, cut once."

2x2

PENCIL MARK ALL AROUND AT INSTRUMENT SIGHT LEVEL

¾-INCH PLYWOOD

Steps in leveling sills:
1. Locate high point.
2. Take reading on ruler.
3. Take reading at each bolt and add ½ inch for grout.
4. Cut wood shim of thickness required at each bolt.
5. Paint cement wash on foundation top to aid bonding of grout.
6. Put mortar bed in place.
7. Put sills on.
8. Finish exposed edges of mortar bed.

1. With sills in place, locate the high point, making sure sill is in contact with foundation.

2. & 3. Take a reading on a ruler and add ½ inch for mortar bed. The bed serves two purposes: A good seal and good support. Do the same at each bolt, making sure ½ inch is added. Record dimensions on sill.

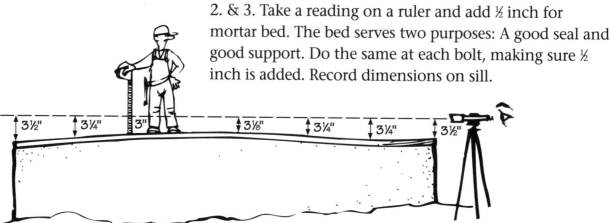

4. Cut shims, 2 inches by 2 inches by thickness required at each bolt.

5. Paint top of foundation with a thin creamy paste of cement and water.

6. & 7. Mix a rich batch of mortar and apply to top of foundation wall. Keep it soft so that the sill will have no trouble compressing it to the level of the shims. Keep the mortar away from shims to make sure it does not ooze over on top, preventing the sill from sitting on the shims.

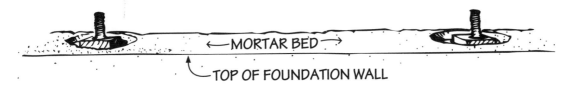

If sill piece is warped, that is, has a bow in it, put the hump up and press it into the mortar with a strong straight edge.

If sill piece has a "crook," sometimes called a "crown" or "wow," it can be used if you snap a chalk line and cut it straight.

8. Clean up squeezed-out mortar, and smooth with trowel.

Grouting the mudsill after it is installed allows the framing to progress. The grouting can then be done at any time; however, there should be easy access to both sides of the sill.

ANCHOR BOLT

MUDSILL

LEVELING SHIM

SHIM SPACER

JOIST HEADER

SHINGLE SHIM

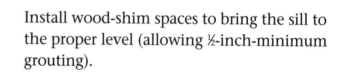

Install wood-shim spaces to bring the sill to the proper level (allowing ½-inch-minimum grouting).

Install mudsill, joists, and headers. Shim mudsill up to joist header where necessary by using narrow strips of wood shingles.

Grout under mudsill by throwing mortar into the space between mudsill and foundation. Push mortar to center with shingle butt. Fill all space under mudsill.

Termite Barrier

Where termites are a problem, a barrier is a must. The best material is 20-ounce copper. Zinc and aluminum will work. Silica-gel, a drying agent, has been used experimentally as a permanent termite control sprinkled around a building during construction. It is extremely absorbent, and when it touches an insect's shell, it eats a hole in it and then goes on to dehydrate the critter. Because insects have exoskeletons, they are the only ones effected by silica-gel. It is totally nontoxic to folks and other animals. I know it works on fleas in a house. It is used to dry flowers, and is used in packaging and in refrigeration.

This termite barrier is the best choice where infestation is bad. It offers the best protection but is the most costly.

This termite barrier is good for most conditions.

This termite deflector is good where infestation is not too bad. It is the least expensive. Use only when top of foundation is easily visible, such as basement areas. Do not use with crawl spaces.

Bending Sheet Metal

2x4

12 to 14" 2x4

Beating on sheet metal with a hammer doesn't make for a neat bend. Setting up like a sheet-metal shop's "brake" helps do a neat job, and it is quicker.

PRESSURE HERE

LONG BEND

MANY SHOTS IN THIS DIRECTION

PRESSURE HERE

FIRST HIT FOR SHORT BEND . . .

. . . WORKING DOWN TO THIS. MANY SHOTS IN THIS POSITION MAKE A NICE FLAT FACE.

Use pieces of whatever length you can handle. Shorter is easier, only it means more seams. Locate the anchor-bolt holes, drill, and put the first piece in place. Lap the next piece (1 inch for copper, 1½ inches for zinc or aluminum), locate bolts, drill, and place on foundation. At corners, lap 1 inch for copper and full lap for zinc or aluminum. When all pieces are in place, clean joints and solder just like copper tubing. If zinc or aluminum is used, a lock seam should be used.

LOCK SEAM

To bend a termite barrier in place, use a block of the required thickness to bend the metal over. It is a good two-man job, but not impossible for one. Always put pressure on a block of wood on top of the sheet to keep it from bulging up. Make bends by beating with a block of wood.

With copper, inside corners are cut, filled with a wedge, and soldered.

With zinc or aluminum, inside corners are cut and the resulting gap filled with a rectangle slipped under and caulked.

Beam pockets should be fully lined.

⏱ Joists and Headers

There are basically two types of framing: "balloon framing," and "platform or Western framing." The exterior wall studs in platform framing are broken at each floor by joists and headers. The studs in the balloon framing are unbroken, with the joists resting on the sill at foundation level and on ledger strips at the other floor levels. The balloon framing is ideal for the energy-conserving house. The exterior walls have unbroken insulation, between the studs, from roof to foundation.

PLATFORM OR WESTERN FRAMING

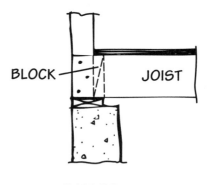

BALLOON FRAMING

An ideal combination is balloon framing with the superinsulated walls. If properly built, superinsulated houses need very little heating other than sunlight through windows, the heat of appliances, lights, and body heat.

Mark an "X" on the crown edge, preferably on each end so you won't have to hunt for it. Use a soft-lead pencil, lumber crayon, or felt-tip pen.

TWO SQUARE ENDS IF BUTTED . . .

←. . . ONE SQUARE END IF LAPPED

Check the ends for square, both ends if you need them.

Always measure from a squared end.

Watch out for pieces of wood or dirt hanging on the end, especially when using a tape measure that hooks over the end.

With the sills square and level, the joist and headers should go in easily. Use straight pieces for headers. If one has a slight crown, it can be pulled down with toenailing.

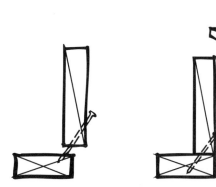

Start with the header a little outside the sill so that when it is driven home, it will be flush. When toenailing, always hit the nail, not the wood. Let the nail do the pulling.

If the header still doesn't line up when the nail is driven home, use another toenail. Really pound those nails. If necessary use three, not too close together; the wood might split.

CROWN DOWN ...   UP ...   STRAIGHT ...   STRAIGHT

Joists should be laid in crown up. The weight of the floor will flatten them out in time. If joists are chosen randomly, there will be high joists next to low joists, making for a very uneven floor.

To find the crown, sight down the length of the "stick" while it is lying on the pile. If you pick up one end, it will sag making a curved sight line.

CROWN SIDE

STRAIGHT   CROOKED

Each end joist should be straightened. The best way to see if an end joist is straight is to stretch a string (Mason's line) from one end to the other over ¾-inch shim blocks at each end. The reason for the shim blocks is to make sure the string does not touch the joist. Slip another ¾-inch block between string and joist, at various points along the joist, and you will see how much out or in it is.

Straighten joist and hold in place with a diagonal brace. Sitting down and pushing with the powerful leg muscles will make any stubborn joist move. Leave the nail heads up for easy removal.

With the header and end joists straight and securely braced, the rest of the joists can be straightened. Take 1x3 furring strips and mark off the joist spacings at the header. Then move the stick 5 or 6 feet away from the header and tack each joist in its proper place. Make sure the strip is at least 50 inches back from the header to allow for one row of plywood. Stay clear of the bridging.

If the sill is straight, then the header will be straight on the bottom; if the joists are square, then the header will be straight on the top.

STRAIGHT HEADER IF JOISTS ARE SQUARE

STRAIGHT SILL

If joists are not square but instead tip in or out, the header will not be straight on top.

NOT AS GOOD

1½"

When marking joist locations on a header, a single line with an "X" on the side against which the joist is to go will do, but many mistakes are made here. The joist is often put on the wrong side. Better to mark both sides of the joist and put an "X" in the middle.

For joist installation by one person, a folded-over nail supplies support at one end while you nail at the other.

10d NAIL

HEADER
JOIST

I've put in 12-foot pressure-treated 2x8s using this system.

Setting joists to a snapped chalk line on the mudsill makes for a straight header and easy installation.

HEADER
JOIST

SILL

SNAPPED CHALK LINE

Solid bridging has a few problems that make it bothersome to put in. It tends to creep or gain if there are problem joists. This requires attention and adjusting. Plumbers don't like this type of bridging (more holes to drill). Most of the time they just knock any block out that gets in the way.

SOLID BRIDGING — JOISTS

DESIRED 16" OR 12" SPACING LINES

Although the mathematical size of the blocking is 14½ inches (for joists 16 inches on center) or 10½ inches (for joists 12 inches on center), cut them a tad short, about ⅟₁₆ inch. And test a few in place. Keep eyeballing down the joists to make sure they are not bowing.

Bridging should not be nailed solid until the building is complete. This allows all the joists to equalize and settle. With solid bridging it is not easy to drive home the top nail after the deck is in place. It is tough enough with a 2x8 at 16 inches on center; imagine a 2x12 at 12 inches on center. You have to swing the hammer in an arc and, at the right time (trial and error), go for the nail.

FRUSTRATING   EASY   AWKWARD

FAT BLOCK   BLOCK SLIPPED DOWN   GOOD

If Sheetrock is to go on the ceiling below with no furring strips (strapping in New England) over the joists, then the blocking must be put in with care. They must not hang below joist bottoms. Chop bottoms off those that do with a hatchet.

CHALK LINE SNAPPED ON JOISTS

Prenail the joist for solid bridging. The top nail is nailed when you are standing on a plank alongside the chalk line marking the center line of the blocking. The blocks are staggered, so stagger the nails. The bottom nails are best nailed from below. Load the plank with blocks and nail them in place with the top nail only. Drive it home hard to pull the block against the joist. The bottom nail is driven home from below when all blocks are in place.

Diagonal Wood Bridging

1x3 or 1x4 wood bridging can be obtained precut at most lumber yards. Cutting it on the job is not too difficult once you set up a jig. The easiest tool for the job is the radial saw, but a Skil-Saw and miter box setup works fine. The simplest way to find the size is to draw it on a piece of scrap joist material.

CUT EQUAL ANGLES

MARKED JOIST

With the angle and length of the bridging known, you can set up a miter box. If the angle is less than 45 degrees, the bridging will have to be cut vertically because a Skil-Saw will not adjust to less than 45 degrees. 1x4 bridging will need a 9-inch Skil-Saw to reach the full depth.

Bridging

BLOCK OF WOOD
AGAINST JOIST
TO GET AN ANGLE
OF CUT #1
EQ.
EQ.

BRIDGING STOCK
PROJECT
LINE UP
SIDE OF
JOIST
CUT #2
EQ.
EQ.

Narrow bays (less than 16 inches on center or 12 inches on center) will have to be cut with a handsaw. Either draw it on a piece of scrap or mark it in place.

Prenail the bridging with two nails on top and two nails on the bottom.

Lay a plank on the joist alongside the chalk line, marking the center line of the bridging. Load up the plank with the prenailed bridging. Nail the top end only.

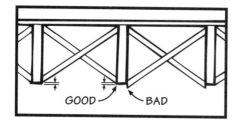

GOOD — BAD

Keep the bottoms of the bridging up a tad from the bottom of the joist for better bearing.

Sometimes there is a problem driving in a block at an angle into a tight place. The top corner digs in and won't move. Beat on this corner with a hammer to round it off. It should at least start easier, but if it still won't go, beat on the corner diagonally opposite.

ROUND EDGE
HERE, TOO, IF NECESSARY

Plywood

Eyeball down the joists to check for straightness. You can pick up errors quickly that way.

Because of today's poor quality control, the plywood sheets should be checked for size. They can be as much as ⅛ inch longer and wider than 48 inches x 96 inches. Combined with the 6d-nail spacing (required) between sheets, this error makes for quite a gain at the end of four sheets. If you don't compensate by gaining a little on the joist spacing, you will have to cut plywood sheets so that they hit halfway on a joist.

Snap a chalk line on top of the joists at 48 inches from the header and lay the plywood sheets to that line. The header may be straight, but the chalk line is straighter. Put a few sheets to walk on, but be sure the ends are supported. Tack the first row in place, leaving the nail heads up for easy removal. Put one nail in each corner to keep the sheets flat. Proceed with a few more rows, tacking and spacing. The reason for tacking is that, no matter how careful you are, the sheets will have to be adjusted to come halfway on a joist. When a few rows have been adjusted and set, drive the "tacked" nails home. This gets rid of the little toe trippers. Lay the rest of the sheets in place, adjust, and tack. Snap chalk lines across the deck on joist center lines. Nail it up.

Adjust plywood sheets by jumping up and in the direction the sheet should go. As you land, drive your feet in the direction of movement. Vary intensity of movement by varying effort. The smaller the effort, the less the movement.

Big effort, big movement . . .

After the deck is on and nailed, it can be easily checked for level with a builder's level (transit) and a wood soldier. It is a good time to set Lally columns, too.

T&G Decking

T&G decking comes in 1-, 2-, 3-, and 4-inch thicknesses (¾, 1½, 2½, and 3½ inches). Try to buy from a good mill or be prepared to struggle getting the pieces together. The 3- and 4-inch types are produced only by the bigger mills. They are also double tongued, so they had better fit well. They are predrilled for large spikes. A heavy hammer or a light maul is a must.

A poor fit is the result of poor milling. The tongue is usually slightly larger than the groove. Sometimes it's the alignment that is out.

Even with the variations involved, all will go together with the proper persuasion. A heavy hammer, prybars, toe nails, and a few tricks will help. If the piece is bowed badly, two prybars can be used alternately to walk the stick in. A combination of any or all can be used.

Keep checking the ends for gain and straightness. Begin measuring from the starting edge to the last board laid. Eyeball down the length for straightness. When past the middle, switch to measuring to the finishing edge.

Gap the weak end to gain a little with each new row. Make sure strong end gets driven home.

If the middle is bowing out, drive it hard and gap the edges. If a constant check is made, the corrections will be minor. A 2-inch surprise with three boards left is not easy to make up.

Even though the sill was squared, another check is in order here. Establish the true outside corners and mark the true inside corners using a block of whatever the exterior wall plate is (2x4, 2x6 . . .). The deck, like the foundation, cannot be changed; so the corners are altered as were the sills. Snap a chalk line connecting the corners, establishing the inside edge of the exterior walls. The walls go to this line regardless of what the deck does. If the sill and joist were done with care, the outside face of the exterior wall should line up pretty well with the outside face of the deck.

EDGE OF DECK

CHALK LINE

STOP - (2) 2x4s NAILED TO DECK

90°

2x4s TO BE CUT

2x4s BELOW KEEP SAW BLADE CLEAR OF DECK

SAW GUIDE

SAW SHOE TO BLADE DIMENSION

The exterior walls are built on the deck, covered with plywood, then tipped up into position. If anything other than plywood is used, diagonal let-in braces must go in each corner.

Most lumber yards will precut studs. They cost more but are worth it. A radial-arm saw on the job does just what the lumber yard does. A power saw with a jig setup on the deck works well not only for studs but also for other multiple cuts. Here is a good time for "measure twice, cut once." I ignored it one time and cut all the exterior studs 12 inches short.

I overcame that error by building a 12-inch wall, using it as the windowsill height and then putting the short stud wall on it.

My short-stud-wall error made me aware of the problems in using a tape measure. It is an ideal tool for a left-handed person because the tape is held in the right hand and the pencil in the left. The tape is then naturally hooked to the left end of the board, extended to the right and read left to right.

7' - 10" (RIGHT DIMENSION)

6' - 10" (12" TOO SHORT)

A righty holds the tape in the left hand, pencil in the right. The natural motion is to hook the tape on the right end of the board and then extend the tape to the left. A righty must then read the unnatural way, right to left. If the tape is hooked on the left end, the righty has to turn the hand over, extend to the right, and cross over with the right hand to mark, all of which is very awkward. This backward reading causes many errors. Six and one-half inches will be read short by going first to the full number and then to the *right* ½ inch for a reading of 5½ inches.

MARK & CUT
2x4 UNDER
LINE UP ENDS
TOP & BOTTOM PLATES

Cut top and bottom plates in pairs.

The top and bottom plates do not have to be on a 48-inch module to accommodate plywood. They can be butted anywhere because the double top plate and the lapped plywood will tie them together.

CORNER CONDITION

1st SECTION

2nd

TOP PLATE

BOTTOM PLATE

±4'-0" (USE ACTUAL SHEET DIMENSION)

THIN LEG OF SQUARE IS 1½"

Mark stud locations on upper and lower plates for the entire wall. To do this, butt all plates together.

Cut sills, headers, trimmers, and cripples for all windows and doors. Code mark and set aside for use as needed. If a radial saw is not available for this, use the jig setup for stud cutting and adjust for the lengths required. To get accurate dimensions for the pieces, draw the locations of the sill and header on a stud. Use blocks of header and sill material. A 2x10 header could measure 9¼ inches to 9½ inches. Two 2x4s should measure 3 inches, but not always. When stacked together, these gains multiply. After cutting one set, check it on the stud.

HEADER

2 CRIPPLES OR TRIMMERS

WINDOW OPENING

DOUBLE OR SINGLE WINDOW SILL

5 CRIPPLES

SILL

STUD

NOTE GRAIN DIRECTION

GLUE AND NAIL AT 4 INCHES ON CENTER

TOP PLATES

INSULATION BETWEEN CRIPPLES AT 16 INCHES ON CENTER

A header does not have to be spaced. Pack out with ½-inch drywall inside.

A good header for an energy-efficient house is an insulated box beam.

If two 2x4s have to be nailed together, it is a good opportunity to use up the crooked ones by opposing the bends. Start at one end and work up the board to the other, toenailing as you go.

Exterior Walls

Snap a line parallel to the deck edge for the length of the building. Nail 2x4 blocks, for stops, on this line. The top plate will be built to these blocks. Three blocks on the edge of the deck will hold the wall square while assembling.

The entire wall is built on the deck. Check the diagonals of the complete wall; they should be equal. Toenail the bottom plate to the deck, driving the top plate hard against the blocks. Leave the nail heads out for easy removal. If sheathing other than plywood is used, let-in diagonal bracing must be used. This is explained in "interior partitions."

Butt the plywood tight, one piece to another. There is no problem of swelling from moisture here, but each section should be gapped to make sure the plates come tight and no wall gain occurs. Be careful not to nail the plates where the plywood overlaps (you can't raise the entire wall in one piece). Window and door openings are marked on the plywood as it goes on. A power saw makes quick work of cutting them out while the wall is still flat on the deck.

DUPLEX NAIL ...   ... DEWPLECK'S SNAIL

For temporary nailing, leave the nail heads out for easy removal; but for better nail-holding power, the duplex nail can't be beat.

WALL BLOCK

NAIL KEEPS BRACE HANDY. BRACE SLIDES ON IT. 2x4 BLOCK LETS BRACE CLEAR TERMITE SHIELD.

NAIL IN THE READY

When the first section of wall is raised, it will have to have a temporary brace. The brace must not interfere with the wall that goes at right angles with it in the corner. A 2x4 spacer block is nailed to the sill below, and a 2x4 block is nailed to the top of the partition. To these blocks the temporary brace is nailed. Nail the 1x3 brace to the wall block and put a nail at the ready in the other end. A nail for the brace to slide on is a great help. Raise the wall section, drive it into position with a sledge, rough plumb, and nail the brace. Before raising the wall, check the bottom plate for nails or pebbles stuck to it. Tack the bottom plate with a few nails, leaving an option to move it. The other sections follow.

Brace the middle sections through the window openings. A diagonal brace nailed to a 2x4 block nailed through the deck into a joist will do. If the sections don't line up because of a dip in the deck, shim them with wood-shingle tips to bring in line.

SHIM HERE

Secure sections together when they are adjusted in place and braced back to the deck, allowing room for building the adjacent walls. Build the adjacent walls the same way. Raise the corner section, drive into position, and tack the bottom plate. The corner is pulled together and tacked. Check for plumb each way. It should be on the money if the panels are square and the deck is level. Once all the walls are in place, the bottom plate should be nailed securely. Make sure to hit the joist and header below.

NAIL BOTTOM PLATE INTO HEADER AND JOISTS IF THERE.

TIGHT STRING ALL AROUND, OUT ON ¾" BLOCKS

BRACES LOCATED SO AS NOT TO INTERFERE WITH INTERIOR PARTITIONS

PLAN AT TOP OF WALL

The exterior walls are now checked for square with the diagonal measurements. Adjustments are best made with a "come along" winch pulling the long diagonal. Finish all the loose ends, and nail loose and missing plywood. It is more efficient if done now and less likely to be forgotten. The walls are straightened with spring braces. Shimmed strings around the perimeter are the guide lines.

A spring brace is a 1"x6"x16' board nailed to the top plate of a wall to be straightened, and to the deck as well. The wall is pulled in by pushing up or bowing the middle of the brace with a 50-inch length of 2x4.

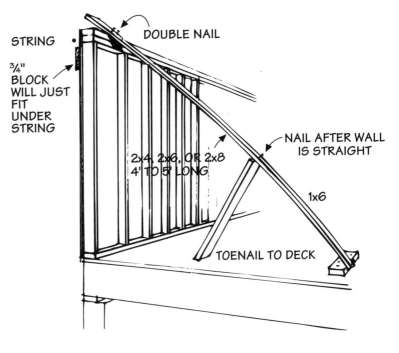

STRING

DOUBLE NAIL

¾" BLOCK WILL JUST FIT UNDER STRING

2x4, 2x6, OR 2x8 4' TO 5' LONG

NAIL AFTER WALL IS STRAIGHT

1x6

TOENAIL TO DECK

Very fine control can be achieved this way, even by one person. Bow the brace, tack in place, and check the string for ¾-inch clearance. The braces have to be checked, as each new one that goes in affects the others. Leave the strings up for periodic checking, but make sure the ¾-inch shims are in at each end.

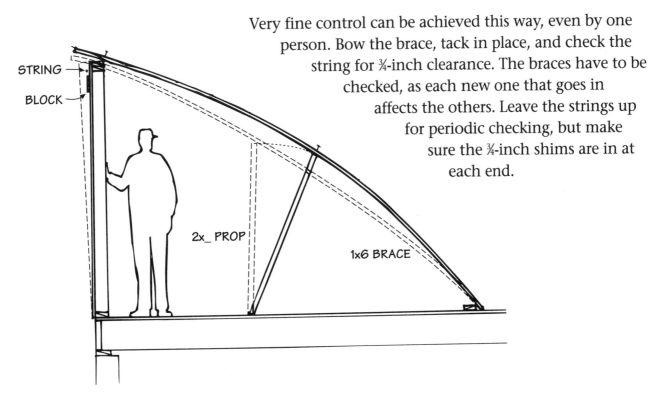

STRING

BLOCK

2x_ PROP

1x6 BRACE

Toenail the bottom plate to the deck to keep the partition from sliding when it is raised.

CHALK LINE LOCATING PARTITION

For spring braces to work properly, the bottom anchor block must be nailed to a pair of joists.

SPRING BRACE

GOOD

← DECK

SPRING BRACE

BAD

← DECK

The bottom of the spring brace should be clear of the deck.

Adjusting the spring brace when the bottom is too close to the deck pulls the nails and loosens the spring brace.

If exterior wall brackets are used, they all go on after the exterior walls are secured straight. The holes in the sheathing for these brackets are drilled in the first stud bay in each corner and spaced to accommodate the staging planks.

WALL BRACKET

2x10

ABOUT 30";
HIGH ENOUGH
SO THAT YOU
CAN GET
ONTO ROOF
SCAFFOLD

(SEE DETAIL)

2x4

2x10s

WOOD STRIP KEEPS
LADDER FROM
PUSHING 2x10s
TOWARD WALL

BLOCK PROTECTS
SIDING

WALL BRACKET

The holes are 30 inches down from the top plate. Staging planks should be no longer than 14 feet. Twelve-foot planks are more comfortable, less bouncy. Drill holes large enough so there is no struggle to get the bracket shaft through. Nail a 1x3 kicker stick on top of the planks so that it reaches over to the siding. This will keep the planks from being pushed in by a heavy ladder load leaning against them. Put a stick wherever a ladder will go. Nail a 1-inch by 3-inch by 18-inch cleat across both planks at the midpoint. It makes the two planks one.

NAIL

2x4

2x4
BLOCK

BLOCK PREVENTS SCAFFOLD FROM
BREAKING 2x4 CROSS PIECE;
NAIL PREVENTS 2x4 FROM
SLIPPING OFF STUDS

If there is to be no plywood deck on the second floor, the exterior walls will have to be permanently stabilized. (The spring braces are only temporary.) The best way to do this is with a 1" by 3" diagonal let-in brace in a perpendicular butting partition. If there is a second floor deck, these partitions can be secured with temporary braces.

INDICATES BRACED PARTITION

PLAN

Build partitions on the deck with let-in braces just tacked in place at the top and bottom plates. Make sure each partition is square and secure before cutting notches for the 1" by 3" diagonal brace. Raise partition into place and secure to exterior wall before double nailing brace to top and bottom plate and each stud. If brace is not let in, and not permanent, tack a diagonal brace on the surface of the partition.

To cut notches, use a power saw set for a ¾-inch-deep cut. With partition square and secure on the deck, tack a guide strip diagonally on partition and cut. Move the guide strip over so that the saw will cut the width of the brace; then cut. Cut in between these two parallel cuts, spacing cuts ¹⁄₁₆-inch to ⅛-inch apart.

It will be easy to break away these thin pieces with a hammer. Clean out bottom of notch with a sharp chisel.

If the standard framing requiring three studs, or blocking and a nailer, at partition intersections is used, a bowed end stud is desirable.

The bowed condition forces the top and bottom plates to be pulled tight against the adjoining partition. Also keep the end stud a tad back from the end of the top and bottom plates.

GOOD   BAD

If drywall corner clips or plywood plates (a floating corner) are used, then a straight stud is a must. This floating corner at an exterior wall intersection is ideal for the energy-efficient house because of its better insulating qualities.

Interior partitions are laid out with chalk lines on the deck. Snap a line for each side of the partition (no guessing where the partition goes that way). Pencil anything that should show up easily and should last.

CHALK LINES

Nail bottom plate to solid wood below, whether joists or blocking.

Plywood alone will sag . . .

CHALK LINE

. . . and partition moves off chalk line too easily.

When one partition intersects another, be sure the end stud is kept back a tad from the end of the top and bottom plates. If it is too strong on the plates, the partition will not come up tight. This is a simple step that takes no extra time.

Use straight studs for door openings; it will make life easier for the "finish" man. Run the cripples to the deck so that the bottom plate butts up to it. Nail two nails into the bottom plate and two at the top, then stagger a nail at each side of the cripple in between. This will keep the 2x4 from twisting, and it leaves a more stable base to shim the door jambs from. Double nailing and alternating sides when face nailing is a good way to keep things solid. If nailed in the middle only, the piece tends to cup and rock.

CRIPPLE

After all the partitions are in and the door openings cut, nail 2x4 blocks (6-to-8-inch scrap) in all the corners and each side of the door openings. This will give good backing for the baseboards.

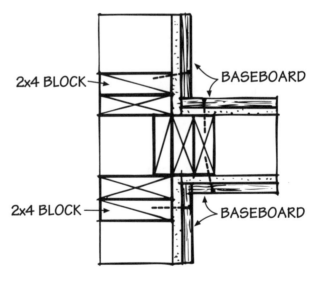

2x4 BLOCK

BASEBOARD

2x4 BLOCK

BASEBOARD

BASEBOARD

DOOR

BASEBOARD

2x4 BLOCK

It has been said that, "a good framer is worth two finish men." If a house is well framed, the finish work goes so easy; if poorly framed, you struggle and fudge over and over.

Rafter lengths and angles are most accurately obtained by drawing them on the deck. If the second floor has no deck, then the place to lay them out is on the first floor— before the walls go up. There are many "rafter rules" and rafter tables that do a fine job. The framing square is another good tool for the job; but if you have a deck to work off, it is foolproof. Make sure that both ends of the deck are equal in length. If rafters are to go alongside joists, this measurement has already been done with the walls below. If there is to be a plate on top of the deck at the edges, snap a chalk line for the plate to nail to.

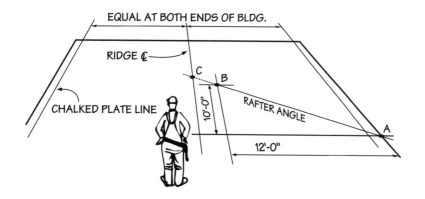

Snap the center line and a base line perpendicular to it. From the roof pitch (10 in 12 for example), establish the angle. Snap a chalk line from point "A" through point "B," crossing center line at point "C." This is the rafter angle. Complete the layout.

Transfer angle, with bevel square or protractor, to a piece of straight rafter stock.

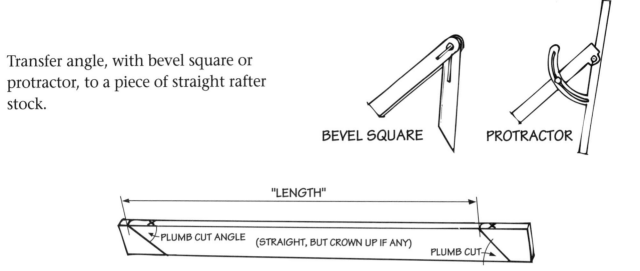

BEVEL SQUARE   PROTRACTOR

"LENGTH"

PLUMB CUT ANGLE   (STRAIGHT, BUT CROWN UP IF ANY)   PLUMB CUT

Mark an "X" on the top to avoid confusion *(even it if is straight)*. Cut the top "plumb cut" only on a pair of straight pieces of rafter stock. Check how they fit over the deck layout. When the fit is good, lay out the rest of the rafter on one piece only. Cut and check with layout on deck. When match is good, cut and mark both pieces with the word PATTERN. Save these "patterns" and two other straight pieces for the end rafters. It will help when trimming with rake boards.

←2x4 DUMMY RIDGE PIECE

PATTERN   PATTERN

EDGE OF BUILDING

CHALKED PLATE LINE

PATTERN

PATTERN

PATTERN . . .

. . . WHATEVER THE STYLE

STOP FASTENED ALONG PENCIL LINE AT PROPER ANGLE
PATTERN
RADIAL SAW
RAIL
SPACE AT END OF STOP AVOIDS SAWDUST BUILDUP
CUT ANGLE

The radial arm saw is the quickest way to cut rafters. Use the "pattern" as a guide for setting the angle and length.

When setting stops, leave a space between rail and stop. This keeps sawdust from building up against the edge, which would change the length of the cut piece.

STOP
RAFTER
RAIL
STOP
RAFTER
RAIL

Cut rafters with crown away from the rail. Avoid using bad pieces; they cause all sorts of problems.

Using an angle T square and tape measure is another way to cut rafters. Best to use a "measuring stick," the length of the rafter, for measuring (hard to read the wrong length on this stick). The T square is made of ¼-inch plywood and a 2x4. Hold it against the rafter (or tack hold), then cut with power saw against the angled edge.

2x4
¼" PLYWOOD
SAW'S SHOE TO BLADE DIMENSION
90°
PLUMB CUT

"LENGTH"
MEASURE STICK
RAFTER
FIRST CUT
SECOND CUT

Still another way is to use the pattern to trace on each piece and cut freehand with power saw or handsaw. The bird's mouth and other cuts are done with a power saw after marking with a jig made up of rafter stock and plywood. Any combination of these can be used.

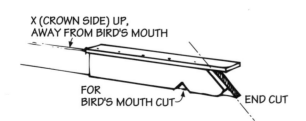

X (CROWN SIDE) UP, AWAY FROM BIRD'S MOUTH
FOR BIRD'S MOUTH CUT
END CUT

PLYWOOD ROOF DECK
RAFTER
2x6 BLOCKS 16" O.C.
FASCIA
1x6 SOFFIT
FRIEZE

If a short overhang is used, blocks cut from the rafter ends can be used (they are the right angle, too). This method creates a nice straight line for the fascia and soffit, and it doesn't matter if there are any irregularities in the rafter ends. It can sometimes mean using the next-shorter-size rafter stock (a 14-footer instead of a 16-footer). Run the blocks through a table saw to even them up in length and width. The blocks are nailed on a 1x6 or 1x8 at rafter locations. Three or four of these sections are made up on the ground.

Locate the bottom of the blocks at each end and at the middle of the building. Stretch a chalk line the length of the building and snap it. If the line is long, hold the string against the wall with your finger, and snap each side of your fingered string. Always finger a long line, particularly on a windy day or if it is on a sidewall. Otherwise, the string will not snap true; also, a long line will not show at the other end of the snap.

EQ.
EQ.
FINGER HERE, SNAP
EQ.
EQ.
SNAP
SNAP

Use a gauge block at each end and in the middle for locating a chalk line.

FURRING STRIP TACKED TO RAFTER
¾"
GAUGE BLOCK

A piece of 1x6 or 1x8 fence board with a U brace at the upper end will support the ridge at one end. Another brace on the deck, fastened to the rafter scaffolding, supports the other. As the rafters go up, the scaffolding is moved along. Scaffolding can also be built the full length of the deck.

SPACE FOR END RAFTER

RIDGE

(2) 1x2s

2x6

1x8

1x2 1x2

1x6, DECK TO RIDGE BOTTOM DIMENSION, LESS ½"

¾" CLEAT W/4 8d NAILS IN EACH BOARD

2 - 2x10s

RIDGE

DECK RIDGE SUPPORT

2x4

1x3s

NAIL

2x4

SIDE VIEW

It is easier to put cleats on top of the planks—no problem with tripping.

2x4s

BLOCK & NAIL

1x3s

2x4s

END VIEW

Cut ridge pieces to fit the length of the building. Lay them on the deck to make sure they are of the correct total length, outside face of stud to outside face of stud. Mark the rafter locations by laying the ridge along the ceiling joists (or the edge plate, if used).

Nail the first end ridge support centered on the face of the end wall. The seat should be ½ inch less than the height of the ridge bottom (dimension on rafter layout on deck). A hand level for plumbing this support will do. The rafter scaffolding, with the short ridge support nailed at one end, should be in place.

With the first ridge piece laid up on the supports, shimmed to the approximate height, one rafter is nailed in place. Shim the ridge to its correct height with the opposite rafter in place. Make sure the straight end pieces you saved are used here.

After the section of rafters is in, it is a good time to plumb the ridge end; but pick a calm day. A moderate wind is okay if there are calm spells. The plumb bob is the best instrument for this job. Loop the string over a nail in the ridge end, then control the bob height with one hand so it just clears the deck and steady it with the other. With the staging moved to the next section, it will be easy to adjust the first section to the plumb position. Secure with a diagonal brace from ridge to deck.

SPLICE BLOCK

The next ridge piece is butted, toenailed, and cleated to the first-section ridge piece. After all rafters are in, they are straightened just like the joists: shimmed string on end-rafter faces, straighten, and diagonal brace. The in-between rafters are eyeballed straight and held with furring strips. A chalk line, fingered in the middle and at 48 inches up from the rafter ends, is snapped for the first row of plywood to be nailed to. Since no water can collect here, the plywood sheets are laid up tight.

48"

Tack the first row to make sure all is going right. If the first row is done right, the rest of the sheets will go well.

Back-prime all exterior trim before cutting it to length to keep it from picking up moisture and cupping severely. The paint will suck into the wood nicely if thinned quite a bit. Paint exposed ends and butted ends to keep moisture out; the trim will last longer. Do not use clear preservative as a primer unless you can wait a few weeks for drying. Paint over preservative takes a long time to dry. If raw wood must go up, put preservative on to keep the surface from drying and cracking. Preservative irritates the eyes, so keep your hands away from your face even long after painting.

PAINTED → ← UNPAINTED

 If unpainted trim sits even a few hours in the sun, it will dry and cup, ultimately splitting.

Stack boards together on edge to paint edges first. Then lay them down for painting the faces.

Space with either thin strips of wood ¼ inch square or 10d nails. Use as many as necessary to keep boards apart.

The garage is a good place to set up painting racks; it's spacious and under cover.

SNAPPED CHALK LINE 36"± OFF FLOOR

2x4 BLOCK

2x6, 8, OR 10

PLYWOOD PAD

SPACED TO KEEP BOARDS FROM SAGGING

STICKERS AT SAG POINT

STICKERS AT BEARING POINTS

Oil-base paint needs good air circulation. ½-inch-square strips for stickers work best.

Painting the edges of a stack of clapboards with a brush speeds up this job.

Painting the faces with a roller (back first then turn board over to roll the face) really speeds things up.

When trimming the exterior of a building, check the ends of the boards for cracks. They will sometimes be very thin lines. If there is a crack, cut off an inch past where the crack begins.

Check the end for poor milling and cut it off.

When butting two pieces of trim, the surfaces sometimes are not flush. Shim the low piece with pieces of 15-lb. felt building paper or wood-shingle tips.

To make good fitting joints on exterior trim, run a handsaw through the joint after the initial cut is made and pieces are tacked in place. It might take two or three cuts. For wood gutters use a very coarse saw. You can't always get a saw into the joints, and in such cases they will have to be trimmed with a sharp block plane.

Check boards for cupping and put the cup face in; the joints stay tighter that way. Wood shrinks on the sapwood or barkside, causing cupping on that surface. In cabinet work the sapwood is kept on the inside surface of the work.

Straight butted ends are cut with the visible face and bottom tight and the back and top open or relieved.

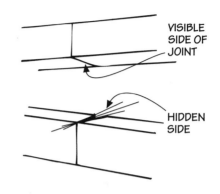

VISIBLE SIDE OF JOINT

HIDDEN SIDE

RELIEVED BACK CORNER
FULL LENGTH OF BOARD

The same principle applies to corner boards wherever one edge butts up to the other face. Use a slight bevel on a table saw or hand plane. Be sure to mark the bevel edge; it's sometimes difficult to tell at a glance.

When planing a bevel on long boards, use a 24-inch jointing plane.

PENCIL MARKS ON BOARD

INSIDE FACE

BEVEL

PENCIL NOTES ON BOARD

When butting boards on a 1½-inch member, use thin wire nails (6d common or 8d box nail), and angle them away from the joint.

1½"

If you must nail close to the edge, dull the nail point with a few hammer blows. A pointed nail pushes the fibers apart, causing a split; but a blunt-end nail tears a hole as it goes through.

Components of Exterior Trim

1. Packing strip for rake members; keep strip short to allow for ear board
2. Fascia
3. Gutter and gutter return with water table
4. Rake boards
5. Soffit
6. Frieze board packing
7. Frieze board
8. Corner boards
9. Miscellaneous trim
10. Ridge boards

ROOF DECK — 1x3 OR 5/4 x3 PACKING STRIP

DOUBLE RAKE BOARDS

15-lb. FELT BUILDING PAPER UNDER PACKING SLIP

SIDE WALL

PACKING STRIP

RAKE BOARD

SHINGLES OR CLAPBOARDS

PACKING STRIP

1. The rake board is packed out so that clapboards and shingles can tuck up behind. A 1x3 furring strip is used if ¾-inch corner boards are used. It is a little tight with shingles that measure ⅞ of an inch from sheathing to face of butts, but it will work (split shakes are much thicker). Use ¾-inch x 3 for ¾-inch corner boards. Yes ¾-inch will work; but the ear board will have to be trimmed to ¾ inch, behind the rake only, to receive it.

2. The fascia is bevel cut on top to match the roof pitch and mitered at one end for ear board return. If rake board covers the corner of ear board and fascia, mitering is not necessary.

ROOF

FASCIA

EAR BOARD

BOTTOM OF RAKE BOARD

PACKING STRIP

RAKE BOARD

BUILDING PAPER

LEVEL FROM BOTTOM OF FASCIA

EAR BOARD

CORNER BOARD

Ear board should be level on the bottom and should have a notch cut in the back to receive the top tongue of the corner board. Paint all cuts.

BACK

(CORNER BOARD)

FACE

¾" CORNER BOARD

¾"

½"

5/16"

CORNER BOARD

½"

¼"

Corner board tucks under ear board.

¾-inch corner board needs ¾-inch ear board with ¼-inch packing strips.

¾" ¼"

¼"± PACKING

½"

¼"

5/4"

TO CLEAR SOFFIT

EAR BOARD

CORNER BOARD

A strip of 15-lb. felt is stapled behind rake and ear board. Use a piece wide enough so that paper on sidewalls can be easily slid under.

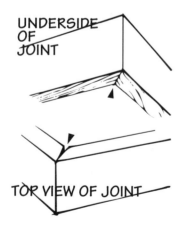

UNDERSIDE OF JOINT

TOP VIEW OF JOINT

Mitering exterior trim with a handsaw is not difficult. The outside corner and the bottom miter line are all that is visible. Start with a good miter cut on the bottom and follow the outside line across the board. At the same time push the saw off the inside line, which will open the inside of the miter cut, making for a good, tight fit outside. If the angle is off, all that has to be adjusted is the small section of the bottom miter.

VERTICAL WOOD STRIPS

10d NAIL 32" ON CENTER

8d NAIL 16" ON CENTER

3. The gutter either returns on the ear board or butts against the rake. In both cases it should be separated from the fascia with wood strips to prevent rotting.

ROOF

FASCIA

GUTTER   10d. NAILS   CHALK LINE

Slope the gutter from middle to ends on long runs. Snap a chalk line and then tack 10d nails on the line to support the gutter while fitting. Sometimes the gable trim limits the slope; just be sure water will not puddle.

FASCIA

EAR BOARD

GUTTER

PLAN

Miter the gutter and the gutter returns in a miter box or freehand. Miter only one end of the return and make sure it is plenty long. Tack in place, level, and inspect the fit. Run a coarse sharp saw through the cut as many times as is necessary for a good fit. Now miter the other end and its little return. The top of the gutter returns will have to be trimmed for the water table to lay flat.

Lead the ends and drill downspout holes with a hole drill in an electric drill or a brace and bit. A nylon plumbing nipple screwed into a hole a tad smaller will not rust out like a galvanized nipple will.

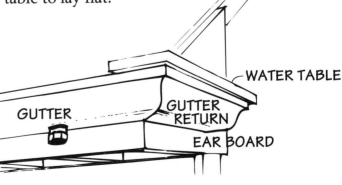

WATER TABLE

GUTTER

GUTTER RETURN

EAR BOARD

Lead laid in gutter up onto roof and water table keeps water out of the gutter return.

LEAD

DOWNSPOUT: 1½" NYLON NIPPLE

PLAN AT END OF GUTTER WITH WATER TABLE AND FLASHING ADDED

ROOF

WATER TABLE

GUTTER

Keep creases out by working lead with hammer handle. Hammer on wood block to tuck lead into corners, being careful not to puncture lead. Use a large piece of lead and trim to fit after shaping. Caulk and nail.

ROOF

RAKE

ROOF

RAKE

WATER TABLE

CAULK SMOOTH

LEAD

GUTTER RETURN

DOWNSPOUT

CAULK EDGE SMOOTH WITH FINGER

LEAD

CAULK UNDERNEATH

WOOD GUTTER

COPPER TACKS

If gutter ends at rake board (no gutter return), treat the same way in gutter and run the lead up to, and lapped on top of, the rake board.

3"

3"

Lead middle mitered joint 3 inches each side of joint.

4. Choose straight boards for the rake if possible. If necessary, however, some bending can be pulled out. With double rake members, the lapped peak is best for tying the whole business together.

FILLER BEHIND
DOUBLE NAIL
NAIL EVERY 5TH COURSE
DOUBLE NAIL PREVENTS TWIST AND CUP KEEPS PIECE FLAT
FINISH NAIL

LAPPED PEAK

TOE NAIL
FILLER BEHIND

PLUMB CUT

Plumb cuts must be cut carefully and nailed securely.

Nail stop blocks on roof and two 16d nails into the side of the building at the bottom line of the rake board. One person can work the rake by resting the board on the nails. Tack in place while getting dimensions and fit.

ROOF DECK
STOP BLOCKS
16d NAILS

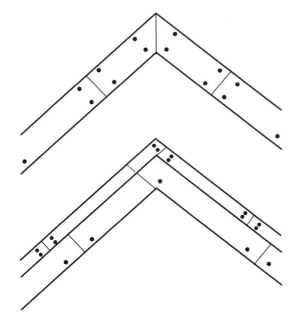

Use a sharp block plane to make the fine fits. If a rake is too long to do in one piece, put the short pieces at the peak end; it's not as visible from the ground. With double members, stagger the joints. Run a handsaw through joints, where possible, to get good joints. Pull rake up to be flush with roof top—strong if anything, not weak. Asphalt shingles look bad sagging down, and wood shingles will split if pulled down too far.

5. The soffit is put on like the fascia. Both ends of each piece are eased back (beveled on the back face).

RAFTER OR BLOCK ENDS

EAR BOARD

SOFFIT — FRONT VIEW

Set all nails used in exterior trim; it pulls the pieces up tight. Putty nail holes before painting. Use your largest nail set for common nails; if stuck without one, use a nail on its side.

Double nail on the bottom. Nail through the fascia as needed.

Wherever the soffit needs pulling in, a pry bar behind is sometimes needed to persuade the piece over. Pull over, nail bottom, then nail front.

WEDGE

2x4

½" PLYWOOD

36"±

BLOCK

STUD

One person can install long sections of trim by using a simple wood L-shaped helper.

HELPER →

WORKING THIS END

FASCIA →

BLOCK

SCREEN

REMOVABLE BLOCK

FLAT BAR →

Nailing the fascia board to soffit when a continuous soffit vent is used works best when it is backed with a removable block spacer and forced over with a flat bar.

6. and 7. The frieze board is packed out with a 1x3 just like the rakes so that the siding tops will fit behind. It's neater and easier, and the shingles won't split and fall out.

FASCIA

USUALLY FILLED W/MOULDING

FRIEZE BOARD

1x3 PACKING

SHINGLES

1x3 PACKING BOARD

CORNER BOARD

Keep the ends in from the corners to allow for the corner board.

8. Fifteen-pound felt spline strips are stapled in place before trim boards are put on. For corners, a piece of building paper (15-lb. felt) is wrapped around the corner extending 4 inches past each corner board on the sides and bottom. Fold the paper down the middle before stapling up. All paper spline strips should be cut at the same time. If you need 144 feet of 12-inch splines (the length of a 15-lb. felt roll), cut it off the end of a roll with a power saw. A 9-inch saw won't quite reach through one-half of the roll. Make sure all lapping paper has the upper piece over the lower piece for water runoff.

15-LB. FELT SPLINE STRIPS

WIDE PIECE | ON FRONT

The narrow corner board piece goes on the side of the building. The wider corner board goes on the face of the building as you look at the front door from the outside.

CORNER BOARD

STOP BLOCK

The narrow corner board piece is nailed on first, keeping it snug against the stops (similar to putting on a rake board). 8d common nails are used for trim nailing with an occasional finish nail and brad.

The wider piece is next. Keep it flush against, and even with, the edge of the narrow one.

4½"

5½"

ROOF

FASCIA

FRIEZE

EAR BOARD

SHIM WITH PAPER IF NOT FLUSH WITH EAR BOARD

NAIL FIRST, THEN DOWN

15-LB. FELT AROUND CORNER

LEAVE PIECES TOO LONG, CUT OFF LATER

Nail at the top first, working down. The wide piece is also nailed at the top, working down at the corner edge only. Make sure the pieces are flush. Then nail the edge that is away from the corner. Set all nails to pull pieces together. Sometimes a 10d common is needed to pull the corners together.

10d NAIL

The wide board usually swells, so a touch up with a sharp block plane will be needed.

The corner boards are left long until after the siding is put on. They are then squared across with a combination square and cut with a handsaw.

9. Miscellaneous trim goes in as needed.

1 2 3

10. The ridge boards are handled just like corner boards except for the angle.

EAR BOARD

FRIEZE

Preassembling corner boards is a good idea whenever installing them.

BOTTOM

TOP

The narrow board should be beveled to create a tight joint at the outside face.

Adjust the tops to reach the ear board and frieze board.

This outside corner has plenty of solid wood for nailing corner boards in place. There is also access for insulating at the corner.

This corner cannot be insulated easily, and the nailing for one of the corner boards is not good.

When building a house, get the roof on as soon as possible, unless you want the summer sun to dry green framing lumber. With the roof on, the building becomes a good place to work and store material out of the weather. With windows and doors installed, the house can also be locked up.

This is a comfortable setup for roofing with either wood or asphalt shingles. The wall-bracket scaffolding is there to start the roof from and provides a good place to keep supplies for the roof work. Later it can be used for loading up the roof scaffolding with shingles.

Red cedar is the best material for a wood-shingle roof. Some people suffer severe infections from red-cedar splinters—nothing to worry about, but be aware.

The first course of a wood-shingled roof is doubled; and if the rake extends to cover a gutter, the starter course is extended. This keeps the rake from weathering.

³⁄₈" GAUGE STICK TACKED TO RAKE BOARD WITH 4d BOX NAILS

NAIL TO RAKE

ELIMINATE IF NO RAKE EXTENSION

NAIL TO FASCIA

7⅞"±
5"
1"
5"±
1"
³⁄₈" 1½" 1"
2⅞"
RAKE BOARD SHINGLE

Put two or four together and cut a nice curve with a coping saw.

GAUGE STICK

ROOF SHINGLES

TEMPORARY ³⁄₈" STRIP

RAKES

Make sure the ⅜-inch-gauge sticks are tacked on the rakes to allow for overhang.

⅜-inch overhang at the rake
1-inch overhang at the eaves

⅛"
1"

Nail the rake-board shingles at each end and one shingle in the middle of the roof. All will be positioned with a 1-inch overhang at the eaves. Stretch a string from end to end and tack below the bottom edge of the shingles. The middle shingle is to support the string in a long span. Keeping the string below the shingle bottom lets the shingles be placed close to, but not touching, the string. If a shingle touches the string, the line moves down; if another touches, the line moves down some more. Eyeball along the bottom to be sure all is well.

Wood shingles are usually laid with 5-to-5¼-inch courses. A roofing stick with shingle gauges is made up with that in mind. The sticks are made of straight 1x3x12-, 14-, or 16-foot furring strips, as many as it takes to reach the length of the roof.

Start with the second course, using the roofing sticks by lining up the bottoms of the shingle gauges with the course below. This will give an automatic 5-inch or 5¼-inch course. Nail the very tip of the gauge to the roof with a wood-shingle nail.

The stick is removed by tapping it with a hammer, which leaves the nail in the roof.

With the sticks secured along the full length of the roof, just lay the shingles with the butts against the 1x3 and nail. Lay as many as is comfortable and then nail, but do not nail the shingle that is over the gauge unless it spans by quite a bit. It will either split or the gauge shingle will get nailed. Make sure the shingles don't slide under the stick. It is very easy to skip a course, so keep checking.

Even though the shingles are wet, space them loosely; don't squeeze them in. Some moisture will be picked up, and they will swell and buckle. If an old batch of very dry shingles is used, ⅛-inch spacing is recommended. Wide shingles should be used; but after nailing them into place, cut the surface where you want them to split. Nail each side of the cut.

THIS . . .   . . . NOT THIS.

Red-cedar shingles are long lasting and a little harder than white cedar. Do not drive the nails hard, just enough to snug the shingle to the roof. On the last stroke, hold back a little. The nail should not be driven below the surface of the shingle or the shingle will crack. Be aware of cracked shingles as you use them. If you are uncertain, bend the shingle; the crack will show. Discard if bad.

There is an up and a down on a shingle; eyeball down the edge and see. The curve is very slight, but it is important to put the hump up. If not, shingles ski up.

"DOWN" FACE

2x8 METAL STRIP BELOW

1"

SPLIT OCCURRED AFTER JOB WAS DONE

1½"

CUT TO CONTROL SPLIT

Shingle joints should be a minimum 1½ inches offset on each course and 1 inch every third course to prevent leaks.

Roof brackets with 2x10 planks for staging are the most comfortable to work from. Locate brackets over rafters for secure nailing. As the staging is advanced up the roof, be aware of the courses into which the brackets must go. Fit the shingle, but leave it out. Tuck the tip under a shingle nearby.

Fifteen-pound felt on the roof under the shingles will further prevent roof leaks. On new work, lay only as much paper as is required for the day's work. An evening moisture will wrinkle the paper severely, making it tough to shingle over.

Check dimensions from eaves to last course, at both ends and middle. Adjust course as necessary, reducing the course if 16-inch shingles are used. If using 18-inch shingles, then an increase will be all right. It is a good idea to snap a chalk line every once in a while to straighten things out. Keep a check, as you get near the ridge, for parallel and shingle-course dimensions. Figure where the bottom of the ridge board will go, then measure to the last shingle course laid to decide on any adjusting needed. A 2-inch final course looks bad.

When the shingling is finished, check the roof for splits that line up and mark with a pencil. Cut some 2x8 metal strips to slip under each split.

NO CUTOUTS

CUTOUTS OR 3-TAB SHINGLE

Asphalt shingles without cutouts are the faster to install and should last longer. The first place to wear on 3-tab shingles is in the cutout.

Wood-shingle starters at the eaves make a nicer looking job than metal strips. The roof is started just like the wood-shingle roof, with a 1-inch wood-shingle overhang. Building paper with lines is a big help in keeping the courses straight; so put the paper on with care, keeping edges running parallel with the eaves.

ASPHALT - ¼" OVERHANG
WOOD SHINGLE - 1" OVERHANG

Measure the length of the roof so that the shingle layout will eliminate a thin shingle strip at the gable ends. With tab shingles, the tabs at each end look best when equal.

All asphalt shingles have marks for alignment. Follow the marks but keep an eye on the paper underneath and adjust to it, provided the paper has been put on parallel to the eaves.

All the starter-course shingles are cut and installed according to the instructions on the bundles. Tack the first asphalt-shingle course in place, with a ¼-inch eave overhang on the wood shingles, according to the layout arrived at earlier. Frequently these layouts turn out wrong and are easier to change if the nails are not driven home. A piece of asphalt shingle has to be cut to cover the rake-board shingle. Make sure the ⅜-inch-gauge strip is tacked on the rake. Too much asphalt-shingle overhang tends to sag.

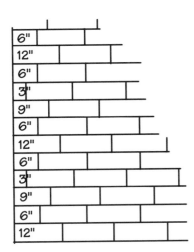

After the shingle layout is established, vertical lines are snapped from ridge to eaves. These offset lines are only used with tab shingles. These lines keep the cutouts aligned up the roof. Shingles without cutouts should be staggered randomly. There is also a random stagger for cutout shingles that looks good.

Roof brackets and 2x10 planks are the most comfortable to work from and good for stacking bundles on. As the ridge is approached, provide for full 5-inch courses all the way. If the paper was laid parallel to the eaves, use it as a guide for straightness, along with an occasional eyeball down the course. A few chalk lines for the last few courses are a must to bring them in line with the ridge. Don't be too fussy on the roof; you can't see the imperfections from the ground. Only at the ridge is it noticeable. Be very concerned with the prevention of leaks.

The gable ends can be either cut off as the course is worked on or cut when finished along a snapped chalk line. The ⅜-inch-gauge strip is used as a guide for cutting as you go. Starter pieces can be cut and worked from one end. If they are cut as you go, lay the shingle in place, reach under and mark with nail, turn over, and cut with knife or tin snips.

Divide a full shingle into thirds to get the cap pattern. Cut the ends away from the butt, tapered, so that, when they fold over the ridge, the corners won't stick out. Take one of the caps and mark PATTERN on it. Lay it on the back side of a full shingle and cut with a utility knife. Use the pattern as a guide for the knife. Keep caps warm for easy folding.

Snap a line for one side of the ridge and nail caps to it. Keep caps warm and install them on a sunny day; the caps will crack if folded over on a cold day. Nail one side of each cap and, if it is warm, bend it over and nail the other side. If not, nail them all on one side and let the sun work for you. Bend and nail when they are warm.

If shingles must be carried up a ladder, carry them on your shoulder.

Tip bundle to groin area. Left hand is to the body side of the center line of the bundle. The right hand is away from the center line.

Drive hips forward and, at the same time, pull with arms to final resting place, the right shoulder.

Any wood can be used for shingles, but in New England white cedar is the first choice because of its beautiful graying quality. Red cedar ages a not-so-pretty brown. Hand-split shakes are usually red cedar and much thicker. Some of what follows applies to clapboards too. White cedars are flat sawn about ⅜ inch at the butt and 16 inches long. When buying shingles, buy a brand name. They might cost a little more, but they will be worth it in time saved. Try a trial bundle or two to see how they go up. They should sit one next to the other, with an occasional trimming required. They might go better right to left or left to right. When you find a good brand, stick with them. They are graded clears and extras, the extras being the better of the two.

BOTTOM OF FRIEZE

34" WINDOW EQUALS 7 ROWS OF SIDING AT 5" MINUS ⅛" PER ROW OR 4⅞"

UNDERSIDE OF SILL

50 ½" EQUALS 10 ROWS OF SIDING AT 5" PLUS ¹⁄₁₆" (-)

BOTTOM OF SIDING

TOP

WDW

BOT.

Mark the various horizontal interruptions the walls have on a story pole. Start with the front of the building.

Mark the corner boards and door casings. Go light with the pencil.

The shingles might need some adjusting around the corner, but usually windows are set at the same height. There might be a short kitchen or bath window. See if the same spacing works.

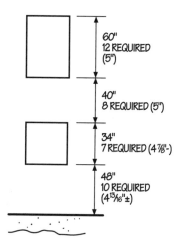

60"
12 REQUIRED
(5")

40"
8 REQUIRED (5")

34"
7 REQUIRED (4⅞"-)

48"
10 REQUIRED
(4¹³⁄₁₆"±)

5"± COURSES

5"± COURSES

WDW.

PINE STRIP
IF 1½" OR
LESS

White cedars are 16 inches, so stretching much past 5 inches loses triple coverage—better to reduce. 5⅛ inches or 5³⁄₁₆ inches will do if indeed the shingles are 16 inches, but many bundles have quite a few "shorts."

Start with building paper stapled to the wall and tucked under the door and corner splines. Keep the bottom of the paper at the bottom edge of the shingles.

PAPER SPLINE

15-LB. FELT (PAPER)

DOUBLE COURSE
ON BOTTOM

SINGLE
COUSES

The shingles can be laid to the bottom of the paper edge or on a 1x3 stick with metal strips hung on the wall.

15-LB. FELT (PAPER)

1x3

METAL STRIP

1x3

Snap a chalk line from corner to corner for the start of the next course. Tack one or two 1x3 furring strips to that chalk line. Use 4d box nails high on the 1x3. The small wire nail won't leave a big hole in the shingle, and, if it is high on the course, it will be less noticeable.

FRIEZE   WINDOW SILL   RAKE

When face-nailing shingles that tuck up under the frieze, windows, or rakes, use galvanized 5d box nails. They look better and hold better if nails are in a straight line and set with a nail set. The shadow line of the frieze, window sill, or rake can be used as a guideline. Otherwise, a light pencil line, with a gauge stick as a guide, will do.

¾" x 1"

SHINGLES DO NOT
QUITE TOUCH

¾" x 1"

TOTAL SHINGLE
THICKNESS: 1"

INSIDE CORNER

On short runs use a level to mark the line for a short 1x3.

For inside corners use ¾x1 to keep shingle butts from clashing. A 1x1 will do, but it will be more noticeable.

1x3

White cedars can be laid up tight; there are no dry ones, so they will shrink. In fact the two last shingles in a course can be angled, like shuffling cards, and snapped in.

snapped 'er too hard again, didn't he?

Trial and error will show how strong the snap can be to make this work.

SCORE WITH SHARP KNIFE

ONE LOOSE NAIL

6" MIN.

1x3

Work both ends to the middle. Two workers, a lefty and a righty, make a good combination. Lap the last pair of shingles, score with a knife, break, and put back in; they should fit. Usually there is a shingle that fits perfectly after a little shave with a sharp knife or hatchet. Shingles should fit against casings, and a block plane helps them fit.

White cedars have "in" and "out" faces. Look for the curve and put the hump out. It's very slight, but it's there.

"IN" FACES

LOAD WITH SHINGLES

SHINGLE TABLE
3 WOOD SHINGLES

A shingle table is used to avoid the need for reaching for shingles when in a difficult position or on a ladder. Two or three tables around the job are all that are needed. Slip the tip under a shingle course and load with shingles.

The first course of wood sidewall shingles can be laid on a 1x3 stick that has a few support, or hanger, shingles nailed to it.

SUPPORT
SHINGLE

1x3

SUPPORT SHINGLE

1x3

STARTER COURSE

The support, or hanger, shingles are permanently nailed in place as one of the underneath starter-course shingles. When the shingling is finished, the 1x3 is removed and the protruding shingle butts are cut off with a handsaw or utility knife.

Many shingles can be set in place before nailing them when a Mason's line is stretched along the tips. Mason's line blocks work well at trim and corners. Finish nails in the trim work as well.

MASON'S BLOCK OR FINISH NAIL

MASON'S LINE

Joint spacing is not critical on sidewalls, but they still should not line up. A 1½-inch minimum at each course should be held. The third course is not too critical.

SILL

MIN. ½" TO MAX. ⅝"

Window sills are usually not rabbeted enough to receive the shingles. Use a ½-inch minimum; a ⅜-inch rabbet is better. Widen the rabbet on all the windows at the same time before installing them.

Use narrow shingles against corners and casings. Wide shingles shrink too much, leaving gaps at these points. Be aware of bad shingles, splits, and bad spots or very hard ones. Discard the hard shingles, they will curl badly and split. Splits in white cedars are generally throwaways.

DORMER CHEEK

USE NARROW SHINGLES AT CORNERS

GABLE

GABLE SHINGLE

DORMER

CHEEK

CHEEK SHINGLE

Save wide shingles ("bedsheets") for gables and dormer cheeks.

Cut all cheek and gable shingles at the same time, it's easy enough to figure how many. A table or radial saw is best for this job, but a handsaw or power saw will cut through a stack of them.

To put in or replace a shingle in a completed shingle wall use a wood wedge, nail set, and box nails. Drive the shingle up to ½ inch from aligning with butts. Use a block, held at the butt, to hammer against. Pry up the shingle above and hold with wedges. Drive two 4d nails at an angle, set nails, and drive shingle to proper alignment. The upper shingle won't bend easily. Shingling up the gable end using metal wall brackets will leave a condition like this at each bracket.

To cut a quantity of shingles to a specific length (for under windows and frieze boards), cut them, while still in the bundle, with a power saw. Drop the bundle on its end to even the butts. Measure size on top of bundle, and count the layers combined with width of bundle for quantity. Eight layers at 20 inches equals 160 inches, or about 13 feet.

20"   5¼"

8 LAYERS

HEADER

BACK VIEW....
⅜" x ⅜" CUTOUT

CAULK

To keep casings water tight, the side casings should be rabbeted into the header. The sills should be caulked.

A clapboard jig is a must for getting good fits at corners, window trim, and door trim. The jig straddles the clapboard and is held hard against the trim while marking a cut line with a utility knife or sharp pencil.

MARK WITH KNIFE

A   B   C

TRIM →   TRIM →

Ⓐ - THE JIG

Ⓑ - THE JIG STRADDLING THE CLAPBOARD AT CORNER OR TRIM

Ⓒ - ANOTHER JIG DESIGN

Secure the building at the end of the day. Take ladders down to prevent the winds from toppling them and to keep kids from climbing them. Batten down the paper that's on the building. That includes all the splines at corners, windows, and doors as well as roof and sidewalls. A strong wind will rip them off in a hurry. Wood-shingle tips, scraps, furring strips, or any scrap sticks tacked to the building will do the job. Tuck loose shingles, whether asphalt or wood, under unopened bundles. Rebind partly used wood-shingle bundles. Pick up paper wrappings and wood-shingle scraps; they love to fly with the wind to the neighbors' yards. There is a bonus to this clean up; many a lost tool is found.

Look over what was done and plan the next day's work. Try to complete each job stage—nailing off the deck, bridging, wall straightening—as you go. It is too easy to forget where you left off. It breaks continuity to have to come back to do this, and it is less efficient. Most of the time, postponed work does not get done. Check for incomplete job stages and plan to finish them the next day. Check the material on hand, and the material required for the next day's work. Double-check for tools left on the job. It is a good way to wind down, to save tools, and to get ready for a good start the next morning.

When winding up extension cords, alternate windings from day to day or week to week. Wind with the right hand one day and the left the next. It is particularly important with rubber cords because they will twist and split. The plastic cords simply get twisted and tangled, making unwinding difficult.

TUESDAYS AND THURSDAYS ...

... MONDAYS, WEDNESDAYS, AND FRIDAYS.

Accidents, both personal and to the tools and building, are always preventable. Never leave a block of wood on the ground with a nail through it.

A good reason not to wear sneakers on the job

Fold it over or, better still, pull it. It won't dull a saw when you're cutting alongside a nail.

Nails are particularly hazardous at the end of long boards. They can rip open a hand or leg even when folded over. Any nails sticking out where there are people can do a job on clothes and skin. Doorways and hallways are not places for projecting nails.

Keep work areas in front of saws clear. Throw cut ends away into a scrap pile. Stumbling over blocks in front of a saw is not only dangerous, it is also aggravating; and when one is aggravated, one gets careless. Keep decks clear of 2x4 blocks; they are great ankle twisters.

Try to prevent wood braces from projecting too far out at about forehead height. It is a height that is easily missed with the eye but easily found with the head.

If a board must be there, hang a flag on it.

Clean up frequently; a clean job is a less accident-prone job.

Don't use tools beyond their capacity. A shovel is not a pry bar.

This is a string-and-shim setup for straightening walls—a simple loop to start at one end and the old-fashioned "butcher's twist" at the other. That's what the old-time butchers used to call it when they tied up their meat.

Pull string tight, then take up slack at nail. If you pull at the nail, the line will break.

If the string is to be pulled very tight, you will have to repeat steps 3 and 4 two or three times to get it to hold.

A ladder is an awkward thing to move, especially one with a long extension. It can be moved quite easily this way, even fully extended. It requires some balancing with arms, body, and head.

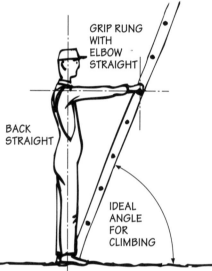

GRIP RUNG WITH ELBOW STRAIGHT

BACK STRAIGHT

IDEAL ANGLE FOR CLIMBING

SETTING UP LADDER — FIREMAN'S WAY

MOVING A HEAVY LADDER FULLY EXTENDED

KEEP FOOT OF LADDER CLOSE TO GROUND

Every once in a while a nail must be located too high or too far from the work platform to be reached with both hands (one for holding the nail, one for the hammer). It can be sunk, though, if the nail is tucked in the claws of the hammer, with the nail head against the hammer neck and the nail pointing out. Some hammers accept a nail this way better than others; wedge the nail in, though, and it should stay. Then reach up and start the nail with a swing. Once it's held firmly by the wood, the hammer is reversed and the nail driven home.

To draw a straight line, the thumb holds the pencil firmly against the pointer and middle fingers. For lines up to one inch from the edge, the middle finger rides along this edge.

For more accurate lines, use the combination square.

Scratch initials on tools for quick identification.

Lines up to four inches from the edge can be drawn using your little finger as the guide. Whatever finger you use, keep them all rigid by bracing them against each other.

Clinching a Nail

To clinch a nail by simply folding it over will work, but a better way is to bend the tip and then fold it over, driving the tip into the wood. Be sure to back up the nail head with a piece of metal to keep the nail from being pushed back out while being folded over.

... BEND THE TIP

COMPLETE THE BEND ...

... FOLD OVER AND DRIVE HOME.

Rough Sharpen & Setting Saw Blade

Even though a good carpenter has a good supply of sharp blades on the job, there is bound to be a time when a blade has to be sharpened on the job. To sharpen, support the blade, as close as possible to the tooth being dressed, and follow the existing angles with a firm forward stroke of the file. After sharpening, lay the blade on a piece of plywood and set every other tooth with a nail set and hammer. Turn the blade over and repeat on that side. The more set there is, the easier and rougher the cut.

There are many problems that crop up on a job that seem to have no solutions. Of course solutions are possible, but you never know where those solutions will come from, so be receptive to ideas. Also be aware of others' problems. You may have the solutions they need.

My dad told me of one situation with a problem that was solved in just that way. He was trimming out a dormer with crown mouldings that met at the rake and eaves. The angle of the cut was impossible to figure. A fellow carpenter below looked up and said, "Eyeball and cut it." So my dad did it, and to his amazement it worked!

Then months later, on another job, the same fellow carpenter who had been below giving the advice was up against the same problem himself and was unable to solve it. This time my dad was below and said to him, "Eyeball and cut it." To the amazement of both parties, it worked again. You never know.

CROWN MOULDING

In concentrating on carpentry tricks of the trade, I have not shown or discussed many safety practices or devices, taking it for granted that basic procedures would be practiced by the reader. Safety goggles, protective clothing, safe ladders, temporary railings, and many other products and practices are part of good carpentry work. OSHA rules, manufacturers' instructions, building codes, and, most of all, common sense must take priority over hammers and nails in successful carpentry.

⊙ Miscellaneous Tips

Cutting flashing is best done with a utility knife. A framing square, held against a partition plate that has been marked off for the flashing size, makes for square cuts of equal length.

Any size nail can be started with this one-hand nailing method.

Hold a nail between the fingers with the nail head against the side of the hammer head. With one brisk swing, drive the point of the nail into the wood.

exploded view of
LOW HORSE
build two...

one at 36", one at 40½"

9" on 40½"
7" on 36" (9" allows 2"
projection for vice
clamp)

7"

5½"

7"

10"

14"

1x6

27½"

13½"

1x6

1x6

½" plywood +
6d box nails

indicates
nail
pattern
(8d common
in 1x6s)
clinch nails

1x6 outside legs on 40½",
1x6 inside legs on 36"
so horses will stack (nest).

CLINCH 6d OR 8d NAILS
IN LEGS. SEE CLINCHING
DETAILS.

OPTIONAL SPLAYED LEGS
some tricky
joint cuts
involved

projection for
vice clamp

2x6

1x6

½"
plywood

1x6

1x6

splay legs if
more stability
is desired.

one horse with 1x6 inside,
one with it out, for stacking.

Saw Horses

HIGH HORSE

one at 36", one at 38½"

54"

26"

±30"

same as height
of low horse

HIGH HORSE . . .
lightweight
and stacked
for easy
transport

(low horse)

LOW HORSES

11½"

There are quite a few
combinations in which these
light-weight horses can be
used.

36" long horse atop 40½" horse gives 11½" added height

Radial Saw Stand and Doghouse Cover

This light-weight portable stand is for a Rockwell 10-inch contractor model saw. Adjust dimensions to fit others.

22" clear

2x4

1¼" angle

¾" pipe

2x4

34"

1¼" angle

RADIAL SAW STAND

1½" floor flange

1½" legs

30"

3"x3"x⅛" plate

36" (front)

2x4

2x4s

1x6

34"

18"

1x6 brace at each support

well-driven stake

pads under

Four wing supports are needed.

nail to supports

nail to saw stand

heavy-duty plug for disconnect and removal at end of day

220 v.

temporary pole

#10 wire

1x3 furring strip rail

wings: (2) 2x8s level with tabltop

½" splice between table and wings

After the stand is set up and wings are attached, eyeballed parallel to the saw's table fence, snap a parallel chalk line from end to end. Nail a 1x3 furring strip, on each wing, to this line. Be sure there is a gap between wings and saw's table to allow for doghouse cover. Make up a length (25 feet or so) of #10 wire, with a heavy-duty plug for the 220V connection to a work pole.

⬡ Radial Saw Stand and Doghouse Cover

RADIAL SAW
FRONT VIEW

heavy-duty plug
for disconnect and
removal at end of day

MOTOR

shim to top
of table

±½" space
for doghouse
cover

two 2x8 wings
level with table top

2x4

1½" floor
flange

1½" leg

clamp saw base to 1¼" angle
to keep from shifting. Use "C" clamps
or bolts if more security is needed.

Remove yoke with motor at end of day unless security is no problem. A heavy-duty plug installed on the wire from the motor makes this easy.

glue with waterproof glue, then paint.

3" aluminum vent each side

top: ¼"
plywood

front
¼" plywood

side
¼" plywood

27"

30"

31"

36"

¾" square

front

1" to rest on
table top

2" to
clear
fence

(rear-end view with plywood removed)

A doghouse cover for the radial saw keeps the elements away. A nail here and there will help secure it.

LADDER
cut both pieces
knot-free 1x3s
³/₈" saw cuts for easy knock out
12"
any reasonable length 2x4. Use knot-free lumber.
2x4
³/₈"
snug fit for 1x3
20"
2x4

One of the first things needed on a job is a ladder. Usually these ladders are 10 or 12 feet, but if a longer one is built, use straight-grained fir for greater strength. Mark and cut both rails at the same time. If you make two, cut all four at the same time.

3'-0"
(2) 2x10s
1x3
½" plywood both sides of 2x4s glued and nailed
3'-0"
2x4 brace
2x4 PUSH BRACKET OR WALL BRACKET
2X4 stake
about 45 degrees

Slip bracket over a long 2x4 and lean it against the building. Set up a matching one and then drive a stake at the base of each diagonal 2x4 brace. The brackets are now ready for the 2x10 planks.

"A" Frame Scaffolding

The wider, the more stable but also the more cumbersome

This scaffolding is cumbersome but effective. A good variation on this is to build just the top part 6 to 8 feet high. Although you can climb up the outside, it is better to use a ladder. Always put wood pads under scaffolding posts and legs to keep them from sinking into the ground.

Tool boxes should have a place for nail sets, block plane, framing square, combination square, chisels, sharpening stone, oil can, hatchet, and level. The level should be protected in a separate compartment. The chisels and hatchet should have their edges protected. A separate box for handsaws is a must, and the blades must be separated from each other. A third catchall box for tools like hammers, nail picks, flat bars, screwdrivers, and wrenches is helpful. This box must be strong enough to handle the heavier weight but not too deep (to prevent piling up of too many tools).

There are many things one can do to keep tools from rattling around.

🔲 Tool Box

Rip all bottoms, ends, and inserts 5½ inches wide. Then rip all sides 5 inches wide, along with partitions as required. Sides and bottoms are all the same length. The handle is two end thicknesses less than the sides. The ends can be simple or fancy. The saw inserts will have to fit your saw lengths. The blades should be clear of the bottom; they stay sharper that way.

A shallow box 3½ inches high and 7 inches wide makes a good one-layer box.